SLOW COOKER DOG FOOD COOKBOOK FOR ROTTWEILER

Dr. Wesley Glasgow

SLOW COOKER DOG FOOD COOKBOOK FOR ROTTWEILER

DISCLAIMER

The content within this book reflects my thoughts, experiences, and beliefs. It is meant for informational and entertainment purposes. While I have taken great care to provide accurate information, I cannot guarantee the absolute correctness or applicability of the content to every individual or situation. Please consult with relevant professionals for advice specific to your needs.

TABLE OF CONTENTS

INTRODUCTION

In the heart of every dog lover lies a story—a tale of companionship, loyalty, and unwavering devotion. For me, that story began with a Rottweiler named Dan. From the moment he entered my life as a wide-eyed pup, I knew our bond would be unbreakable. Little did I know, our journey together would ignite a passion that would shape the course of my life forever.

As a child, I revelled in the joy of having Dan, a Rottweiler, by my side. His playful antics and boundless energy brought laughter and light into our home. But amidst the joy, there lurked a shadow—a shadow cast by the consequences of my naivety.

You see, in my innocence and boundless affection for Dan, I made a grave mistake—I fed him anything and everything I could find. From table scraps to indulgent treats, Dan's diet knew no bounds. It wasn't until years later, as Dan's health began to deteriorate, that I realized the gravity of my folly.

The signs were subtle at first—a slight lethargy here, a few extra pounds there. But as time wore on, Dan's condition worsened. He became increasingly listless, his once vibrant spirit dimmed by the weight of his failing health. It was a heartbreaking sight—one that spurred me into action.

With a heavy heart and a sense of urgency, I sought the counsel of a veterinarian. The diagnosis was devastating—Dan had developed diabetes, a condition exacerbated by his poor diet and sedentary lifestyle. In that moment, I was overcome with guilt and remorse. How could I have allowed this to happen? How could I have failed him so miserably?

But amidst the despair, there flickered a glimmer of hope—a beacon of light illuminating the path forward. Through diligent research and unwavering determination, I discovered the transformative power of nutrition. I learned that food was not just sustenance; it was medicine—a potent elixir capable of healing and rejuvenating even the most ailing souls.

And so began my journey—a journey fueled by a relentless desire to right the wrongs of the past and forge a brighter future for dogs like Dan. Armed with newfound knowledge and a fervent passion for canine nutrition, I embarked on a quest to revolutionize Rottweiler health—one slow-cooked meal at a time.

Today, after 25 years of tireless dedication, I stand before you not only as a veterinarian but as a seasoned cook with a wealth of experience and wisdom. My name is Dr. Wesley Glasgow, and I am honored to share with you the culmination of my life's work—a slow cooker dog food cookbook tailored specifically for Rottweilers.

In the pages that follow, you will find a treasure trove of meticulously crafted recipes designed to nourish, heal, and rejuvenate your beloved Rottweiler. Each recipe is a testament to the power of good nutrition—a testament to the profound bond we share with our furry companions.

But this cookbook is more than just a collection of recipes; it's a beacon of hope for Rottweiler owners seeking to enhance the health and vitality of their canine companions. It's a testament to the resilience of the human spirit and the transformative power of love.

As you embark on this culinary journey with me, consider the questions that linger in the recesses of your mind. How does your Rottweiler's diet impact their overall health and longevity? What are the dangers and consequences of unhealthy eating habits for dogs? And most importantly, how can this cookbook serve as a catalyst for positive change in your Rottweiler's life?

Within these pages, you will find not only delicious and nourishing recipes but also the keys to unlocking a brighter, healthier future for your cherished Rottweiler. Together, let us embark on a journey towards Rottweiler rejuvenation—a journey guided by love, compassion, and the transformative power of good nutrition.

With every meal prepared with care and love, may your Rottweiler thrive and flourish, embodying the vibrant spirit and boundless joy that define this magnificent breed. Welcome to the beginning of a new chapter—a chapter filled with health, happiness, and endless tail wags. Welcome to the "Slow Cooker Dog Food Cookbook for Rottweiler: A Journey to Optimal Health

Contact the Author

Thank you for reading my book! I would love to hear from you, whether you have feedback, questions, or just want to share your thoughts. Your feedback means a lot to me and helps me improve as a writer.

Please don't hesitate to reach out to me through

glasgowesley@gmail.com

I look forward to connecting with my readers and appreciate your support in this literary journey. Your thoughts and comments are valuable to me.

CHAPTER 1

Understanding Your Rottweiler's Dietary Needs

Rottweilers, known for their strength, loyalty, and robust appearance, require a balanced and appropriate diet to maintain their health and vitality. Understanding their specific dietary needs is essential for ensuring their well-being and longevity. In this guide, we'll delve into Rottweiler health essentials, common dietary issues, and how to tailor meals to meet your Rottweiler's individual requirements.

Rottweiler Health Essentials:

1. **Protein Requirements:** Rottweilers are muscular dogs with high protein requirements to support their active lifestyle. Opt for high-quality animal-based proteins such as lean meats (chicken, turkey, beef), fish, and eggs to promote muscle development and maintenance.

2. **Healthy Fats:** Incorporating healthy fats into your Rottweiler's diet is crucial for maintaining skin and coat health, as well as supporting overall wellness. Sources of healthy fats include fish oil, flaxseed oil, and coconut oil.

3. **Complex Carbohydrates:** While Rottweilers don't have a high carbohydrate requirement, incorporating complex carbohydrates such as whole grains, vegetables, and fruits can provide essential nutrients, fiber, and energy.

4. **Vitamins and Minerals:** Ensure your Rottweiler's diet is well-balanced and includes essential vitamins and minerals like calcium, phosphorus, vitamin

D, and vitamin E to support bone health, immune function, and overall vitality.

5. **Hydration:** Adequate hydration is vital for Rottweilers, especially during hot weather or after physical activity. Always provide fresh, clean water and monitor their intake to prevent dehydration.

Common Dietary Issues in Rottweilers:

1. **Obesity:** Rottweilers are prone to obesity, which can lead to various health issues such as joint problems, heart disease, and decreased lifespan. Monitor their calorie intake, avoid overfeeding, and ensure they get regular exercise to maintain a healthy weight.

2. **Food Allergies:** Some Rottweilers may develop food allergies or sensitivities to certain ingredients such as grains, poultry, or dairy. Watch for symptoms like itching, gastrointestinal upset, or skin issues, and consult your veterinarian if you suspect an allergy.

3. **Gastric Dilatation-Volvulus (GDV):** Also known as bloat, GDV is a serious condition that commonly affects large, deep-chested breeds like Rottweilers. To reduce the risk, feed your Rottweiler smaller, more frequent meals, avoid strenuous exercise immediately after eating, and consider using elevated feeding bowls.

Tailoring Meals to Your Rottweiler's Needs:

1. **Consult with a Veterinarian:** Every Rottweiler is unique, and their dietary needs may vary based on factors such as age, activity level, and health status. Consult with your veterinarian to develop a tailored feeding plan that meets your Rottweiler's specific requirements.

2. **Monitor Body Condition:** Regularly assess your Rottweiler's body condition score and adjust their diet accordingly. Aim for a lean, muscular physique with a visible waistline and minimal fat covering the ribs.

3. **Rotate Protein Sources:** Incorporate a variety of protein sources into your Rottweiler's diet to ensure they receive a diverse range of nutrients. Rotate between lean meats, fish, and poultry to keep meals interesting and nutritionally balanced.

4. **Offer Nutrient-Rich Treats:** Choose nutrient-rich treats made from high-quality ingredients to supplement your Rottweiler's diet without adding excess calories or compromising their health goals.

By understanding your Rottweiler's dietary needs and implementing a tailored feeding plan, you can help support their health, energy, and overall well-being for years to come. Remember to prioritize high-quality ingredients, portion control, and regular veterinary check-ups to ensure your Rottweiler thrives on a nutritious diet.

CHAPTER 2
Getting Started with Slow Cooking for Your Rottweiler

Slow cooking can be a fantastic way to provide wholesome and nutritious meals for your Rottweiler. By taking the time to cook their food slowly, you can ensure that they receive all the essential nutrients they need to thrive. In this guide, we'll explore how to get started with slow cooking for your Rottweiler, including choosing the right ingredients, essential tips, and safety precautions to keep in mind.

Choosing the Right Ingredients:

1. Protein: Start with a high-quality source of protein such as lean meats like chicken, turkey, beef, or lamb. Make sure to remove any bones and excess fat before cooking.

2. Carbohydrates: Incorporate healthy carbohydrates like brown rice, sweet potatoes, quinoa, or barley to provide energy and fiber.

3. Vegetables: Include a variety of dog-safe vegetables such as carrots, peas, green beans, spinach, and broccoli for added vitamins and minerals.

4. Supplements: Consider adding supplements like fish oil or calcium to ensure your Rottweiler receives all necessary nutrients.

Tips for Slow Cooking Dog Food:

1. Use a slow cooker: Invest in a reliable slow cooker or crockpot to make the cooking process easier and more convenient.

2. Follow recipes: Start with simple recipes designed specifically for slow-cooking dog food to ensure balanced nutrition.

3. Monitor portion sizes: Pay attention to portion sizes to prevent overfeeding or underfeeding your Rottweiler.

4. Incorporate variety: Rotate ingredients and recipes to provide a diverse range of nutrients and flavors.

5. Gradual transition: If switching from commercial dog food to homemade slow-cooked meals, transition gradually over several days to avoid digestive upset.

Safety Precautions:

1. Avoid toxic ingredients: Refrain from using ingredients like onions, garlic, grapes, raisins, chocolate, and xylitol, as they can be toxic to dogs.

2. Cook thoroughly: Ensure all ingredients are cooked thoroughly to kill any harmful bacteria and make them easier to digest.

3. Store properly: Store any leftover food in airtight containers in the refrigerator for up to three days or freeze for longer-term storage.

4. Supervise feeding: Always supervise your Rottweiler while they eat and consult with your veterinarian if you have any concerns about their diet or health.

CHAPTER 3

Breakfast and Brunch Ideas

Chicken and Sweet Potato Hash

Cooking Time: 6-8 hours on low

Servings: 4

Ingredients:

- 2 cups diced chicken breast

- 2 cups diced sweet potatoes

- 1 cup diced carrots

- 1 cup diced green beans

- 1 cup low-sodium chicken broth

Instructions:

1. Wash and dice the chicken breast, sweet potatoes, carrots, and green beans.

2. Place all the diced ingredients into the slow cooker.

3. Pour the low-sodium chicken broth over the ingredients in the slow cooker.

4. Stir the ingredients thoroughly to ensure they are evenly distributed and coated with the broth.

5. Set the slow cooker to low heat and cover with the lid. Allow it to cook for 6-8 hours, or until the chicken is thoroughly cooked and the vegetables are tender.

6. Once cooked, use a ladle to portion the chicken and sweet potato hash into appropriate servings for your Rottweiler. Allow it to cool before serving.

Nutritional Information: Protein: 25g, Fat: 8g, Carbohydrates: 20g, Fiber: 5g, Calories: 250 per serving (serving size: 1 cup)

Turkey and Vegetable Omelette

Cooking Time: 4-6 hours on low

Servings: 6

Ingredients:

- 2 cups cooked ground turkey
- 1 cup diced zucchini
- 1 cup diced bell peppers
- 1 cup shredded carrots
- 6 eggs
- 1/2 cup low-sodium chicken broth

Instructions:

1. Cook the ground turkey until fully cooked. Dice the zucchini, bell peppers, and shred the carrots.

2. In a mixing bowl, crack the eggs and whisk them together with the low-sodium chicken broth until well combined.

3. Add the cooked ground turkey and diced vegetables into the egg mixture. Stir until all ingredients are evenly distributed.

4. Pour the combined mixture into the slow cooker, making sure it spreads evenly.

5. Set the slow cooker to low heat and cover with the lid. Allow the omelette to cook for 4-6 hours, or until the eggs are fully set.

6. Once cooked, carefully slice the omelette into wedges using a knife. Serve the wedges to your Rottweiler in appropriate portion sizes.

Nutritional Information: Protein: 30g, Fat: 12g, Carbohydrates: 10g, Fiber: 3g, Calories: 280 per serving (serving size: 1 wedge)

Beef and Barley Breakfast Stew

Cooking Time: 8-10 hours on low

Servings: 6

Ingredients:

- 2 cups cubed beef stew meat
- 1 cup pearl barley
- 1 cup diced sweet potatoes
- 1 cup diced carrots
- 4 cups low-sodium beef broth

Instructions:

1. Cut the beef stew meat into small cubes. Dice the sweet potatoes and carrots into bite-sized pieces.

2. Place the cubed beef stew meat, pearl barley, diced sweet potatoes, and carrots into the slow cooker.

3. Pour the low-sodium beef broth over the ingredients in the slow cooker.

4. Stir the ingredients thoroughly to ensure they are evenly combined and coated with the broth.

5. Set the slow cooker to low heat and cover with the lid. Allow the stew to cook for 8-10 hours, or until the beef is tender and the barley is cooked.

6. Once cooked, ladle the beef and barley stew into serving bowls for your Rottweiler. Allow it to cool slightly before serving.

Nutritional Information: Protein: 28g, Fat: 10g, Carbohydrates: 35g, Fiber: 8g, Calories: 320 per serving (serving size: 1 cup)

Salmon and Spinach Frittata

Cooking Time: 4-6 hours on low

Servings: 6

Ingredients:

- 2 cups cooked salmon, flaked
- 2 cups chopped spinach
- 6 eggs
- 1/2 cup low-sodium chicken broth

Instructions:

1. Cook the salmon until fully cooked, then flake it into small pieces.
2. Chop the spinach into fine pieces.
3. In a mixing bowl, crack the eggs and whisk them together with the low-sodium chicken broth until well combined.
4. Add the cooked salmon and chopped spinach into the egg mixture. Stir until all ingredients are evenly distributed.
5. Pour the combined mixture into the slow cooker, making sure it spreads evenly.
6. Set the slow cooker to low heat and cover with the lid. Allow the frittata to cook for 4-6 hours, or until the eggs are fully set.
7. Once cooked, carefully cut the frittata into wedges using a knife. Serve the wedges to your Rottweiler in appropriate portion sizes.

Nutritional Information: Protein: 35g, Fat: 15g, Carbohydrates: 5g, Fiber: 2g, Calories: 300 per serving (serving size: 1 wedge)

Turkey and Quinoa Breakfast Bowl

Cooking Time: 2-3 hours on low

Servings: 4

Ingredients:

- 2 cups cooked ground turkey
- 1 cup cooked quinoa
- 1 cup diced tomatoes
- 1 cup diced cucumbers
- 1/4 cup chopped parsley

Instructions:

1. Cook the ground turkey until fully cooked.

2. Cook the quinoa according to package instructions.

3. Dice the tomatoes and cucumbers into small pieces.

4. In the slow cooker, layer the cooked ground turkey, cooked quinoa, diced tomatoes, diced cucumbers, and chopped parsley.

5. Set the slow cooker to low heat and cover with the lid. Allow it to cook for 2-3 hours.

6. Once cooked, serve the turkey and quinoa breakfast bowl to your Rottweiler in appropriate portion sizes.

Nutritional Information: Protein: 25g, Fat: 8g, Carbohydrates: 20g, Fiber: 5g, Calories: 250 per serving (serving size: 1 cup)

Chicken and Pumpkin Breakfast Casserole

Cooking Time: 4-6 hours on low

Servings: 6

Ingredients:

- 2 cups cooked chicken, shredded
- 1 cup canned pumpkin puree
- 1 cup diced apples
- 1 cup cooked brown rice
- 6 eggs

Instructions:

1. Cook the chicken until fully done, then shred it into small pieces.

2. Dice the apples into small chunks.

3. In a mixing bowl, combine the shredded chicken, pumpkin puree, diced apples, cooked brown rice, and eggs. Mix well until everything is evenly incorporated.

4. Pour the mixture into the slow cooker, spreading it out evenly.

5. Set the slow cooker to low heat and cover with the lid. Allow the casserole to cook for 4-6 hours, or until the eggs are fully set.

6. Once cooked, cut the casserole into squares using a knife. Serve the squares to your Rottweiler in appropriate portion sizes.

Nutritional Information: Protein: 30g, Fat: 12g, Carbohydrates: 25g, Fiber: 6g, Calories: 290 per serving (serving size: 1 square)

Beef and Potato Breakfast Stew

Cooking Time: 8-10 hours on low

Servings: 6

Ingredients:

- 2 cups cubed beef stew meat
- 2 cups diced potatoes
- 1 cup diced carrots
- 1 cup diced celery
- 4 cups low-sodium beef broth

Instructions:

1. Cube the beef stew meat into small pieces.

2. Dice the potatoes, carrots, and celery into bite-sized chunks.

3. In the slow cooker, combine the cubed beef stew meat, diced potatoes, carrots, celery, and low-sodium beef broth.

4. Mix everything together until well combined.

5. Set the slow cooker to low heat and cover with the lid. Allow the stew to cook for 8-10 hours, or until the beef is tender and the vegetables are cooked through.

6. Once cooked, serve the beef and potato breakfast stew to your Rottweiler in appropriate portion sizes.

Nutritional Information: Protein: 28g, Fat: 10g, Carbohydrates: 35g, Fiber: 8g, Calories: 320 per serving (serving size: 1 cup)

Turkey and Lentil Breakfast Soup

Cooking Time: 6-8 hours on low

Servings: 6

Ingredients:

- 2 cups cooked ground turkey

- 1 cup dried lentils, rinsed

- 1 cup diced sweet potatoes

- 1 cup diced carrots

- 6 cups low-sodium chicken broth

Instructions:

1. Cook the ground turkey until fully cooked.

2. Rinse the dried lentils under cold water.

3. In the slow cooker, combine the cooked ground turkey, rinsed lentils, diced sweet potatoes, carrots, and low-sodium chicken broth.

4. Stir everything together until well combined.

5. Set the slow cooker to low heat and cover with the lid. Allow the soup to cook for 6-8 hours, or until the lentils and vegetables are tender.

6. Once cooked, serve the turkey and lentil breakfast soup to your Rottweiler in appropriate portion sizes.

Nutritional Information: Protein: 32g, Fat: 10g, Carbohydrates: 30g, Fiber: 10g, Calories: 310 per serving (serving size: 1 cup)

Salmon and Potato Breakfast Bake

Cooking Time: 4-6 hours on low

Servings: 6

Ingredients:

- 2 cups cooked salmon, flaked
- 2 cups diced potatoes
- 1 cup diced green beans
- 1 cup diced bell peppers
- 6 eggs

Instructions:

1. Cook the salmon until fully cooked, then flake it into small pieces.
2. Dice the potatoes, green beans, and bell peppers into small chunks.
3. In a mixing bowl, beat the eggs until well blended.
4. Add the cooked salmon, diced potatoes, green beans, and bell peppers into the beaten eggs. Mix until all ingredients are evenly distributed.
5. Pour the mixture into the slow cooker, spreading it out evenly.
6. Set the slow cooker to low heat and cover with the lid. Allow the breakfast bake to cook for 4-6 hours, or until the eggs are fully set and the potatoes are tender.
7. Once cooked, cut the breakfast bake into squares using a knife. Serve the squares to your Rottweiler in appropriate portion sizes.

Nutritional Information: Protein: 28g, Fat: 12g, Carbohydrates: 20g, Fiber: 4g, Calories: 280 per serving (serving size: 1 square)

Pork and Vegetable Breakfast Stew

Cooking Time: 8-10 hours on low

Servings: 6

Ingredients:

- 2 cups cubed pork loin
- 1 cup diced potatoes
- 1 cup diced carrots
- 1 cup diced green beans
- 4 cups low-sodium vegetable broth

Instructions:

1. Cube the pork loin into small pieces.

2. Dice the potatoes, carrots, and green beans.

3. In the slow cooker, combine the cubed pork loin, diced potatoes, carrots, green beans, and low-sodium vegetable broth.

4. Stir well to mix all the ingredients evenly.

5. Set the slow cooker to low heat and cover with the lid. Allow the stew to cook for 8-10 hours, or until the pork is tender and the vegetables are cooked through.

6. Once cooked, serve the pork and vegetable breakfast stew to your Rottweiler in appropriate portion sizes.

Nutritional Information: Protein: 26g, Fat: 8g, Carbohydrates: 30g, Fiber: 7g, Calories: 290 per serving (serving size: 1 cup)

OTHER BOOKS BY THE AUTHOR

INSTANT POT DOG FOOD COOKBOOK

DOG FOOD COOKBOOK FOR PICKY EATERS

AIR FRYER DOG FOOD COOKBOOK

SLOW COOKER DOG FOOD COOKBOOK

DOG FOOD COOKBOOK FOR SENSITIVE STOMACH

SCAN THE QR CODE TO SEE MORE BOOKS BY AUTHOR

CHAPTER 4

Nourishing Soups and Stews

Beef and Vegetable Soup

Cooking Time: 6-8 hours on low

Servings: 6

Ingredients:

- 2 cups cubed beef stew meat
- 1 cup diced potatoes
- 1 cup diced carrots
- 1 cup diced green beans
- 4 cups low-sodium beef broth

Instructions:

1. Cube the beef stew meat into small pieces.
2. Dice the potatoes, carrots, and green beans.
3. In the slow cooker, combine the cubed beef stew meat, diced potatoes, carrots, green beans, and low-sodium beef broth.
4. Stir well to mix all the ingredients evenly.
5. Set the slow cooker to low heat and cover with the lid. Allow the soup to cook for 6-8 hours, or until the beef is tender and the vegetables are cooked through.
6. Once cooked, serve the beef and vegetable soup to your Rottweiler in appropriate portion sizes.

Nutritional Information: Protein: 25g, Fat: 8g, Carbohydrates: 20g, Fiber: 5g, Calories: 250 per serving (serving size: 1 cup)

Chicken and Rice Soup

Cooking Time: 4-6 hours on low

Servings: 6

Ingredients:

- 2 cups diced chicken breast
- 1 cup cooked brown rice
- 1 cup diced carrots
- 1 cup diced celery
- 4 cups low-sodium chicken broth

Instructions:

1. Dice the chicken breast into small pieces.
2. Cook the brown rice according to package instructions.
3. Dice the carrots and celery.
4. In the slow cooker, combine the diced chicken breast, cooked brown rice, diced carrots, diced celery, and low-sodium chicken broth.
5. Stir well to mix all the ingredients evenly.
6. Set the slow cooker to low heat and cover with the lid. Allow the soup to cook for 4-6 hours, or until the chicken is cooked through and the vegetables are tender.
7. Once cooked, serve the chicken and rice soup to your Rottweiler in appropriate portion sizes.

Nutritional Information: Protein: 20g, Fat: 6g, Carbohydrates: 15g, Fiber: 3g, Calories: 200 per serving (serving size: 1 cup)

Turkey and Barley Stew

Cooking Time: 8-10 hours on low

Servings: 6

Ingredients:

- 2 cups cooked ground turkey
- 1 cup pearl barley
- 1 cup diced sweet potatoes
- 1 cup diced carrots
- 4 cups low-sodium turkey or chicken broth

Instructions:

1. Cook the ground turkey until fully cooked.

2. Rinse the pearl barley under cold water.

3. Dice the sweet potatoes and carrots into small pieces.

4. In the slow cooker, combine the cooked ground turkey, rinsed pearl barley, diced sweet potatoes, diced carrots, and low-sodium broth.

5. Stir well to mix all the ingredients evenly.

6. Set the slow cooker to low heat and cover with the lid. Allow the stew to cook for 8-10 hours, or until the barley is tender and the vegetables are cooked through.

7. Once cooked, serve the turkey and barley stew to your Rottweiler in appropriate portion sizes.

Nutritional Information: Protein: 22g, Fat: 7g, Carbohydrates: 18g, Fiber: 4g, Calories: 220 per serving (serving size: 1 cup)

Salmon and Vegetable Chowder

Cooking Time: 4-6 hours on low

Servings: 6

Ingredients:

- 2 cups cooked salmon, flaked

- 2 cups diced potatoes

- 1 cup diced carrots

- 1 cup diced zucchini

- 4 cups low-sodium fish or vegetable broth

Instructions:

1. Cook the salmon until fully cooked, then flake it into small pieces.

2. Dice the potatoes, carrots, and zucchini into small chunks.

3. In the slow cooker, combine the cooked salmon, diced potatoes, carrots, zucchini, and low-sodium broth.

4. Stir well to mix all the ingredients evenly.

5. Set the slow cooker to low heat and cover with the lid. Allow the chowder to cook for 4-6 hours, or until the vegetables are tender.

6. Once cooked, serve the salmon and vegetable chowder to your Rottweiler in appropriate portion sizes.

Nutritional Information: Protein: 24g, Fat: 9g, Carbohydrates: 20g, Fiber: 5g, Calories: 240 per serving (serving size: 1 cup)

Beef and Lentil Soup

Cooking Time: 6-8 hours on low

Servings: 6

Ingredients:

- 2 cups cubed beef stew meat
- 1 cup dried lentils, rinsed
- 1 cup diced potatoes
- 1 cup diced carrots
- 4 cups low-sodium beef broth

Instructions:

1. Cube the beef stew meat into small pieces.
2. Rinse the dried lentils under cold water.
3. Dice the potatoes and carrots into small chunks.
4. In the slow cooker, combine the cubed beef stew meat, rinsed lentils, diced potatoes, carrots, and low-sodium beef broth.
5. Stir well to mix all the ingredients evenly.
6. Set the slow cooker to low heat and cover with the lid. Allow the soup to cook for 6-8 hours, or until the beef is tender and the lentils are cooked through.
7. Once cooked, serve the beef and lentil soup to your Rottweiler in appropriate portion sizes.

Nutritional Information: Protein: 26g, Fat: 8g, Carbohydrates: 20g, Fiber: 6g, Calories: 250 per serving (serving size: 1 cup)

Chicken and Vegetable Stew

Cooking Time: 4-6 hours on low

Servings: 6

Ingredients:

- 2 cups diced chicken breast
- 1 cup diced potatoes
- 1 cup diced carrots
- 1 cup diced celery
- 4 cups low-sodium chicken broth

Instructions:

1. Dice the chicken breast into small pieces.
2. Dice the potatoes, carrots, and celery.
3. In the slow cooker, combine the diced chicken breast, diced potatoes, carrots, celery, and low-sodium chicken broth.
4. Stir well to mix all the ingredients evenly.
5. Set the slow cooker to low heat and cover with the lid. Allow the stew to cook for 4-6 hours, or until the chicken is cooked through and the vegetables are tender.
6. Once cooked, serve the chicken and vegetable stew to your Rottweiler in appropriate portion sizes.

Nutritional Information: Protein: 22g, Fat: 6g, Carbohydrates: 18g, Fiber: 4g, Calories: 220 per serving (serving size: 1 cup)

Turkey and Pumpkin Soup

Cooking Time: 6-8 hours on low

Servings: 6

Ingredients:

- 2 cups cooked ground turkey

- 1 cup canned pumpkin puree

- 1 cup diced potatoes

- 1 cup diced carrots

- 4 cups low-sodium turkey or chicken broth

Instructions:

1. Cook the ground turkey until fully cooked.

2. Dice the potatoes and carrots into small pieces.

3. In the slow cooker, combine the cooked ground turkey, canned pumpkin puree, diced potatoes, diced carrots, and low-sodium broth.

4. Stir well to mix all the ingredients evenly.

5. Set the slow cooker to low heat and cover with the lid. Allow the soup to cook for 6-8 hours, or until the vegetables are tender.

6. Once cooked, serve the turkey and pumpkin soup to your Rottweiler in appropriate portion sizes.

Nutritional Information: Protein: 24g, Fat: 7g, Carbohydrates: 20g, Fiber: 5g, Calories: 230 per serving (serving size: 1 cup)

Salmon and Lentil Stew

Cooking Time: 8-10 hours on low

Servings: 6

Ingredients:

- 2 cups cooked salmon, flaked
- 1 cup dried lentils, rinsed
- 1 cup diced sweet potatoes
- 1 cup diced zucchini
- 4 cups low-sodium fish or vegetable broth

Instructions:

1. Cook the salmon until fully cooked, then flake it into small pieces.
2. Rinse the dried lentils under cold water.
3. Dice the sweet potatoes and zucchini into small chunks.
4. In the slow cooker, combine the cooked salmon, rinsed lentils, diced sweet potatoes, diced zucchini, and low-sodium broth.
5. Stir well to mix all the ingredients evenly.
6. Set the slow cooker to low heat and cover with the lid. Allow the stew to cook for 8-10 hours, or until the lentils are tender and the vegetables are cooked through.
7. Once cooked, serve the salmon and lentil stew to your Rottweiler in appropriate portion sizes.

Nutritional Information: Protein: 26g, Fat: 9g, Carbohydrates: 20g, Fiber: 6g, Calories: 250 per serving (serving size: 1 cup)

Beef and Vegetable Barley Soup

Cooking Time: 6-8 hours on low

Servings: 6

Ingredients:

- 2 cups cubed beef stew meat
- 1 cup pearl barley
- 1 cup diced potatoes
- 1 cup diced carrots
- 4 cups low-sodium beef broth

Instructions:

1. Cube the beef stew meat into small pieces.

2. Rinse the pearl barley under cold water.

3. Dice the potatoes and carrots into small chunks.

4. In the slow cooker, combine the cubed beef stew meat, rinsed pearl barley, diced potatoes, carrots, and low-sodium beef broth.

5. Stir well to mix all the ingredients evenly.

6. Set the slow cooker to low heat and cover with the lid. Allow the soup to cook for 6-8 hours, or until the beef is tender and the barley is cooked through.

7. Once cooked, serve the beef and vegetable barley soup to your Rottweiler in appropriate portion sizes.

Nutritional Information: Protein: 28g, Fat: 10g, Carbohydrates: 25g, Fiber: 7g, Calories: 270 per serving (serving size: 1 cup)

Chicken and Quinoa Chowder

Cooking Time: 4-6 hours on low

Servings: 6

Ingredients:

- 2 cups diced chicken breast
- 1 cup cooked quinoa
- 1 cup diced potatoes
- 1 cup diced carrots
- 4 cups low-sodium chicken broth

Instructions:

1. Dice the chicken breast into small pieces.
2. Cook the quinoa according to package instructions.
3. Dice the potatoes and carrots into small chunks.
4. In the slow cooker, combine the diced chicken breast, cooked quinoa, diced potatoes, carrots, and low-sodium chicken broth.
5. Stir well to mix all the ingredients evenly.
6. Set the slow cooker to low heat and cover with the lid. Allow the chowder to cook for 4-6 hours, or until the chicken is cooked through and the vegetables are tender.
7. Once cooked, serve the chicken and quinoa chowder to your Rottweiler in appropriate portion sizes.

Nutritional Information: Protein: 24g, Fat: 8g, Carbohydrates: 20g, Fiber: 5g, Calories: 240 per serving (serving size: 1 cup)

CHAPTER 5
Wholesome Main Courses

Beef and Sweet Potato Stew

Cooking Time: 8-10 hours on low

Servings: 6

Ingredients:

- 2 cups cubed beef stew meat
- 2 cups diced sweet potatoes
- 1 cup diced green beans
- 4 cups low-sodium beef broth

Instructions:

1. Cube the beef stew meat into small pieces.
2. Peel and dice the sweet potatoes, carrots, and green beans.
3. In the slow cooker, combine the cubed beef stew meat, diced sweet potatoes, carrots, green beans, and low-sodium beef broth.
4. Stir to mix all the ingredients evenly.
5. Set the slow cooker to low heat and cover with the lid. Allow the stew to cook for 8-10 hours, or until the beef is tender and the vegetables are cooked through.
6. Once cooked, serve the beef and sweet potato stew to your Rottweiler in appropriate portion sizes.

Nutritional Information: Protein: 26g, Fat: 8g, Carbohydrates: 20g, Fiber: 5g, Calories: 250 per serving (serving size: 1 cup)

Chicken and Brown Rice Casserole

Cooking Time: 4-6 hours on low

Servings: 6

Ingredients:

- 2 cups diced chicken breast
- 1 cup cooked brown rice
- 1 cup diced sweet potatoes
- 1 cup diced carrots
- 4 cups low-sodium chicken broth

Instructions:

1. Dice the chicken breast into small pieces.
2. Cook the brown rice according to package instructions.
3. Peel and dice the sweet potatoes and carrots.
4. In the slow cooker, combine the diced chicken breast, cooked brown rice, diced sweet potatoes, carrots, and low-sodium chicken broth.
5. Mix well to ensure all ingredients are evenly distributed.
6. Set the slow cooker to low heat and cover with the lid. Allow the casserole to cook for 4-6 hours, or until the chicken is cooked through and the vegetables are tender.
7. Once cooked, serve the chicken and brown rice casserole to your Rottweiler in appropriate portion sizes.

Nutritional Information: Protein: 22g, Fat: 6g, Carbohydrates: 18g, Fiber: 4g, Calories: 220 per serving (serving size: 1 cup)

Turkey and Vegetable Medley

Cooking Time: 6-8 hours on low

Servings: 6

Ingredients:

- 2 cups cooked ground turkey
- 2 cups diced potatoes
- 1 cup diced carrots
- 1 cup diced zucchini
- 4 cups low-sodium turkey or chicken broth

Instructions:

1. Cook the ground turkey until fully cooked.

2. Peel and dice the potatoes and carrots.

3. Dice the zucchini into small pieces.

4. In the slow cooker, combine the cooked ground turkey, diced potatoes, carrots, zucchini, and low-sodium broth.

5. Stir well to mix all the ingredients evenly.

6. Set the slow cooker to low heat and cover with the lid. Allow the medley to cook for 6-8 hours, or until the vegetables are tender.

7. Once cooked, serve the turkey and vegetable medley to your Rottweiler in appropriate portion sizes.

Nutritional Information: Protein: 24g, Fat: 7g, Carbohydrates: 20g, Fiber: 5g, Calories: 230 per serving (serving size: 1 cup)

Salmon and Quinoa Delight

Cooking Time: 4-6 hours on low

Servings: 6

Ingredients:

- 2 cups cooked salmon, flaked
- 1 cup cooked quinoa
- 1 cup diced sweet potatoes
- 1 cup diced green beans
- 4 cups low-sodium fish or vegetable broth

Instructions:

1. Cook the salmon until fully cooked, then flake it into small pieces.
2. Cook the quinoa according to package instructions.
3. Peel and dice the sweet potatoes.
4. Trim and chop the green beans.
5. In the slow cooker, combine the cooked salmon, cooked quinoa, diced sweet potatoes, green beans, and low-sodium broth.
6. Mix well to ensure all ingredients are evenly distributed.
7. Set the slow cooker to low heat and cover with the lid. Allow the delight to cook for 4-6 hours, or until the vegetables are tender.
8. Once cooked, serve the salmon and quinoa delight to your Rottweiler in appropriate portion sizes.

Nutritional Information: Protein: 26g, Fat: 9g, Carbohydrates: 20g, Fiber: 6g, Calories: 250 per serving (serving size: 1 cup)

Beef and Lentil Casserole

Cooking Time: 6-8 hours on low

Servings: 6

Ingredients:

- 2 cups cubed beef stew meat
- 1 cup dried lentils, rinsed
- 1 cup diced potatoes
- 1 cup diced carrots
- 4 cups low-sodium beef broth

Instructions:

1. Cube the beef stew meat into small pieces.
2. Rinse the dried lentils under cold water.
3. Peel and dice the potatoes and carrots.
4. In the slow cooker, combine the cubed beef stew meat, rinsed lentils, diced potatoes, carrots, and low-sodium beef broth.
5. Stir well to mix all the ingredients evenly.
6. Set the slow cooker to low heat and cover with the lid. Allow the casserole to cook for 6-8 hours, or until the beef is tender and the lentils are cooked through.
7. Once cooked, serve the beef and lentil casserole to your Rottweiler in appropriate portion sizes.

Nutritional Information: Protein: 28g, Fat: 10g, Carbohydrates: 25g, Fiber: 7g, Calories: 270 per serving (serving size: 1 cup)

Turkey and Vegetable Stew

Cooking Time: 8-10 hours on low

Servings: 6

Ingredients:

- 2 cups cooked ground turkey

- 2 cups diced potatoes

- 1 cup diced carrots

- 1 cup diced celery

- 4 cups low-sodium turkey or chicken broth

Instructions:

1. Cook the ground turkey until fully cooked.

2. Peel and dice the potatoes, carrots, and celery.

3. In the slow cooker, combine the cooked ground turkey, diced potatoes, carrots, celery, and low-sodium broth.

4. Stir well to mix all the ingredients evenly.

5. Set the slow cooker to low heat and cover with the lid. Allow the stew to cook for 8-10 hours, or until the vegetables are tender.

6. Once cooked, serve the turkey and vegetable stew to your Rottweiler in appropriate portion sizes.

Nutritional Information: Protein: 24g, Fat: 7g, Carbohydrates: 20g, Fiber: 5g, Calories: 230 per serving (serving size: 1 cup)

Salmon and Potato Bake

Cooking Time: 4-6 hours on low

Servings: 6

Ingredients:

- 2 cups cooked salmon, flaked
- 2 cups diced potatoes
- 1 cup diced carrots
- 1 cup diced broccoli
- 4 cups low-sodium fish or vegetable broth

Instructions:

1. Cook the salmon until fully cooked, then flake it into small pieces.

2. Peel and dice the potatoes and carrots.

3. Chop the broccoli into small florets.

4. In the slow cooker, combine the cooked salmon, diced potatoes, carrots, broccoli, and low-sodium broth.

5. Mix well to ensure all ingredients are evenly distributed.

6. Set the slow cooker to low heat and cover with the lid. Allow the bake to cook for 4-6 hours, or until the vegetables are tender.

7. Once cooked, serve the salmon and potato bake to your Rottweiler in appropriate portion sizes.

Nutritional Information: Protein: 26g, Fat: 9g, Carbohydrates: 20g, Fiber: 6g, Calories: 250 per serving (serving size: 1 cup)

Chicken and Vegetable Stir-Fry

Cooking Time: 4-6 hours on low

Servings: 6

Ingredients:

- 2 cups diced chicken breast
- 1 cup sliced bell peppers
- 1 cup sliced mushrooms
- 1 cup sliced zucchini
- 4 cups low-sodium chicken broth

Instructions:

1. Dice the chicken breast into small pieces.

2. Slice the bell peppers, mushrooms, and zucchini.

3. In the slow cooker, combine the diced chicken breast, sliced bell peppers, mushrooms, zucchini, and low-sodium broth.

4. Stir well to mix all the ingredients evenly.

5. Set the slow cooker to low heat and cover with the lid. Allow the stir-fry to cook for 4-6 hours, or until the chicken is cooked through and the vegetables are tender.

6. Once cooked, serve the chicken and vegetable stir-fry to your Rottweiler in appropriate portion sizes.

Nutritional Information: Protein: 22g, Fat: 6g, Carbohydrates: 18g, Fiber: 4g, Calories: 220 per serving (serving size: 1 cup)

Beef and Pumpkin Stew

Cooking Time: 6-8 hours on low

Servings: 6

Ingredients:

- 2 cups cubed beef stew meat
- 2 cups canned pumpkin puree
- 1 cup diced potatoes
- 1 cup diced carrots
- 4 cups low-sodium beef broth

Instructions:

1. Cube the beef stew meat into small pieces.

2. Peel and dice the potatoes and carrots.

3. In the slow cooker, combine the cubed beef stew meat, canned pumpkin puree, diced potatoes, carrots, and low-sodium beef broth.

4. Stir well to mix all the ingredients evenly.

5. Set the slow cooker to low heat and cover with the lid. Allow the stew to cook for 6-8 hours, or until the beef is tender and the vegetables are cooked through.

6. Once cooked, serve the beef and pumpkin stew to your Rottweiler in appropriate portion sizes.

Nutritional Information: Protein: 26g, Fat: 8g, Carbohydrates: 20g, Fiber: 5g, Calories: 240 per serving (serving size: 1 cup)

Turkey and Barley Casserole

Cooking Time: 8-10 hours on low

Servings: 6

Ingredients:

- 2 cups cooked ground turkey
- 1 cup pearl barley
- 1 cup diced sweet potatoes
- 1 cup diced carrots
- 4 cups low-sodium turkey or chicken broth

Instructions:

1. Cook the ground turkey until fully cooked.
2. Rinse the pearl barley under cold water.
3. Peel and dice the sweet potatoes and carrots.
4. In the slow cooker, combine the cooked ground turkey, rinsed pearl barley, diced sweet potatoes, carrots, and low-sodium broth.
5. Stir well to mix all the ingredients evenly.
6. Set the slow cooker to low heat and cover with the lid. Allow the casserole to cook for 8-10 hours, or until the barley is tender and the vegetables are cooked through.
7. Once cooked, serve the turkey and barley casserole to your Rottweiler in appropriate portion sizes.

Nutritional Information: Protein: 24g, Fat: 7g, Carbohydrates: 20g, Fiber: 5g, Calories: 230 per serving (serving size: 1 cup)

CHAPTER 6

Delicious Treats and Snacks

Chicken and Sweet Potato Bites

Cooking Time: 4 hours on low

Servings: 12

Ingredients:

- 2 cups diced chicken breast
- 2 cups diced sweet potatoes
- 1 cup rolled oats
- 4 cups low-sodium chicken broth

Instructions:

1. Dice the chicken breast and sweet potatoes into small pieces.
2. In a mixing bowl, combine the diced chicken, sweet potatoes, rolled oats, and low-sodium chicken broth.
3. Mix well to ensure all ingredients are evenly distributed.
4. Transfer the mixture to the slow cooker.
5. Set the slow cooker to low heat and cover with the lid. Allow the bites to cook for 4 hours.
6. Once cooked, remove the mixture from the slow cooker and let it cool.
7. Use a spoon or cookie cutter to shape the mixture into bite-sized pieces.
8. Serve the chicken and sweet potato bites to your Rottweiler as a tasty treat.

Nutritional Information: Protein: 10g, Fat: 3g, Carbohydrates: 8g, Fiber: 2g, Calories: 100 per serving (serving size: 2 bites)

Beef and Carrot Jerky

Cooking Time: 6 hours on low

Servings: 10

Ingredients:

- 2 cups thinly sliced beef
- 1 cup diced carrots
- 1/2 cup unsweetened applesauce
- 1 tablespoon honey

Instructions:

1. Thinly slice the beef into strips.
2. Dice the carrots into small pieces.
3. In a mixing bowl, combine the thinly sliced beef, diced carrots, unsweetened applesauce, and honey.
4. Mix well to coat the beef and carrots evenly.
5. Transfer the mixture to the slow cooker.
6. Set the slow cooker to low heat and cover with the lid. Allow the jerky to cook for 6 hours.
7. Once cooked, remove the jerky from the slow cooker and let it cool.
8. Cut the jerky into smaller pieces using kitchen shears or a knife.
9. Serve the beef and carrot jerky to your Rottweiler as a delicious snack.

Nutritional Information: Protein: 8g, Fat: 2g, Carbohydrates: 5g, Fiber: 1g, Calories: 70 per serving (serving size: 1 ounce)

Turkey and Pumpkin Biscuits

Cooking Time: 3 hours on low

Servings: 20 biscuits

Ingredients:

- 2 cups cooked ground turkey

- 1 cup canned pumpkin puree

- 2 cups whole wheat flour

- 1 egg

Instructions:

1. Preheat your slow cooker on low heat.

2. In a mixing bowl, combine the cooked ground turkey, canned pumpkin puree, whole wheat flour, and egg.

3. Knead the mixture until it forms a dough-like consistency.

4. Roll out the dough on a floured surface to about 1/4 inch thickness.

5. Use cookie cutters to cut out shapes from the dough.

6. Place the biscuits on a parchment-lined slow cooker insert.

7. Cover the slow cooker and cook the biscuits for 3 hours on low heat.

8. Once cooked, remove the biscuits from the slow cooker and let them cool completely.

9. Store the turkey and pumpkin biscuits in an airtight container.

Nutritional Information: Protein: 4g, Fat: 2g, Carbohydrates: 10g, Fiber: 2g, Calories: 80 per biscuit

Salmon and Spinach Muffins

Cooking Time: 4 hours on low

Servings: 12 muffins

Ingredients:

- 2 cups cooked salmon, flaked
- 2 cups chopped spinach
- 1 cup grated carrots
- 2 cups whole wheat flour
- 2 eggs

Instructions:

1. Preheat your slow cooker on low heat.

2. In a mixing bowl, combine the cooked salmon, chopped spinach, grated carrots, whole wheat flour, and eggs.

3. Mix well until all ingredients are thoroughly combined.

4. Spoon the mixture into greased muffin cups, filling each about 2/3 full.

5. Place the muffin tray into the slow cooker.

6. Cover the slow cooker and cook the muffins for 4 hours on low heat.

7. Once cooked, remove the muffins from the slow cooker and let them cool before serving.

Nutritional Information: Protein: 6g, Fat: 3g, Carbohydrates: 8g, Fiber: 2g, Calories: 90 per muffin

Chicken and Blueberry Cookies

Cooking Time: 3 hours on low

Servings: 24 cookies

Ingredients:

- 2 cups cooked chicken, shredded
- 1 cup blueberries
- 1 cup rolled oats
- 1/4 cup unsweetened applesauce
- 1 egg

Instructions:

1. Preheat your slow cooker on low heat.

2. In a mixing bowl, combine the cooked chicken, blueberries, rolled oats, unsweetened applesauce, and egg.

3. Mix well until all ingredients are thoroughly combined.

4. Drop spoonfuls of the mixture onto a parchment-lined slow cooker insert, forming cookies.

5. Cover the slow cooker and cook the cookies for 3 hours on low heat.

6. Once cooked, remove the cookies from the slow cooker and let them cool completely.

7. Store the chicken and blueberry cookies in an airtight container.

Nutritional Information: Protein: 4g, Fat: 2g, Carbohydrates: 6g, Fiber: 1g, Calories: 60 per cookie

Beef and Cheese Bites

Cooking Time: 4 hours on low

Servings: 12

Ingredients:

- 2 cups diced beef

- 1 cup grated cheese (use dog-safe cheese)

- 1 cup rolled oats

- 1/4 cup unsweetened applesauce

- 1 egg

Instructions:

1. Preheat your slow cooker on low heat.

2. In a mixing bowl, combine the diced beef, grated cheese, rolled oats, unsweetened applesauce, and egg.

3. Mix well until all ingredients are thoroughly combined.

4. Roll the mixture into small balls and place them on a parchment-lined slow cooker insert.

5. Cover the slow cooker and cook the bites for 4 hours on low heat.

6. Once cooked, remove the bites from the slow cooker and let them cool before serving.

Nutritional Information: Protein: 8g, Fat: 4g, Carbohydrates: 6g, Fiber: 1g, Calories: 90 per bite

Turkey and Cranberry Bars

Cooking Time: 3 hours on low

Servings: 12 bars

Ingredients:

- 2 cups cooked ground turkey

- 1 cup dried cranberries

- 1 cup whole wheat flour

- 1/4 cup unsweetened applesauce

- 1 egg

Instructions:

1. Preheat your slow cooker on low heat.

2. In a mixing bowl, combine the cooked ground turkey, dried cranberries, whole wheat flour, unsweetened applesauce, and egg.

3. Mix well until all ingredients are thoroughly combined.

4. Press the mixture evenly into a greased slow cooker insert.

5. Cover the slow cooker and cook the bars for 3 hours on low heat.

6. Once cooked, remove the bars from the slow cooker and let them cool before slicing into individual bars.

Nutritional Information: Protein: 6g, Fat: 3g, Carbohydrates: 8g, Fiber: 1g, Calories: 80 per bar

Salmon and Peanut Butter Balls

Cooking Time: 4 hours on low

Servings: 12 balls

Ingredients:

- 2 cups cooked salmon, flaked

- 1 cup peanut butter (use unsalted and unsweetened)

- 1 cup rolled oats

- 1/4 cup unsweetened applesauce

- 1 egg

Instructions:

1. Preheat your slow cooker on low heat.

2. In a mixing bowl, combine the cooked salmon, peanut butter, rolled oats, unsweetened applesauce, and egg.

3. Mix well until all ingredients are thoroughly combined.

4. Roll the mixture into small balls and place them on a parchment-lined slow cooker insert.

5. Cover the slow cooker and cook the balls for 4 hours on low heat.

6. Once cooked, remove the balls from the slow cooker and let them cool before serving.

Nutritional Information: Protein: 8g, Fat: 6g, Carbohydrates: 6g, Fiber: 1g, Calories: 100 per ball

Chicken and Pumpkin Muffins

Cooking Time: 3 hours on low

Servings: 12 muffins

Ingredients:

- 2 cups cooked chicken, shredded
- 1 cup canned pumpkin puree
- 1 cup whole wheat flour
- 1/4 cup unsweetened applesauce
- 1 egg

Instructions:

1. Preheat your slow cooker on low heat.

2. In a mixing bowl, combine the cooked chicken, canned pumpkin puree, whole wheat flour, unsweetened applesauce, and egg.

3. Mix well until all ingredients are thoroughly combined.

4. Spoon the mixture into greased muffin cups, filling each about 2/3 full.

5. Place the muffin tray into the slow cooker.

6. Cover the slow cooker and cook the muffins for 3 hours on low heat.

7. Once cooked, remove the muffins from the slow cooker and let them cool before serving.

Nutritional Information: Protein: 6g, Fat: 3g, Carbohydrates: 8g, Fiber: 2g, Calories: 90 per muffin

Beef and Carrot Biscuits

Cooking Time: 4 hours on low

Servings: 20 biscuits

Ingredients:

- 2 cups diced beef

- 1 cup grated carrots

- 1 cup whole wheat flour

- 1/4 cup unsweetened applesauce

- 1 egg

Instructions:

1. Preheat your slow cooker on low heat.

2. In a mixing bowl, combine the diced beef, grated carrots, whole wheat flour, unsweetened applesauce, and egg.

3. Mix well until all ingredients are thoroughly combined.

4. Roll out the dough on a floured surface to about 1/4 inch thickness.

5. Use cookie cutters to cut out shapes from the dough.

6. Place the biscuits on a parchment-lined slow cooker insert.

7. Cover the slow cooker and cook the biscuits for 4 hours on low heat.

8. Once cooked, remove the biscuits from the slow cooker and let them cool before serving.

Nutritional Information: Protein: 4g, Fat: 2g, Carbohydrates: 6g, Fiber: 1g, Calories: 70 per biscuit

CHAPTER 7
Special Dietary Considerations
Dogs with Specific Needs

Sensitive Stomach Turkey Stew

Cooking Time: 6 hours on low

Servings: 8

Ingredients:

- 2 cups cooked ground turkey

- 1 cup cooked brown rice

- 1 cup chopped pumpkin

- 1 cup diced carrots

- 4 cups low-sodium chicken broth

Instructions:

1. Cook the ground turkey and brown rice separately.

2. Chop the pumpkin and dice the carrots.

3. In the slow cooker, combine the cooked ground turkey, cooked brown rice, chopped pumpkin, diced carrots, and low-sodium chicken broth.

4. Mix well to combine all ingredients.

5. Set the slow cooker to low heat and cook for 6 hours.

6. Once cooked, allow the stew to cool before serving to your Rottweiler.

Nutritional Information: Protein: 20g, Fat: 5g, Carbohydrates: 15g, Fiber: 3g,

Calories: 180 per serving (serving size: 1 cup)

Senior Dog Chicken and Rice Casserole

Cooking Time: 4 hours on low

Servings: 6

Ingredients:

- 2 cups cooked shredded chicken

- 1 cup cooked white rice

- 1 cup chopped spinach

- 1 cup diced sweet potatoes

- 4 cups low-sodium chicken broth

Instructions:

1. Cook the shredded chicken and white rice separately.

2. Chop the spinach and dice the sweet potatoes.

3. In the slow cooker, combine the cooked shredded chicken, cooked white rice, chopped spinach, diced sweet potatoes, and low-sodium chicken broth.

4. Mix well to combine all ingredients.

5. Set the slow cooker to low heat and cook for 4 hours.

6. Once cooked, allow the casserole to cool before serving to your senior Rottweiler.

Nutritional Information: Protein: 18g, Fat: 4g, Carbohydrates: 12g, Fiber: 2g, Calories: 150 per serving (serving size: 1 cup)

Weight Management Turkey and Vegetable Stew

Cooking Time: 6 hours on low

Servings: 8

Ingredients:

- 2 cups cooked ground turkey

- 1 cup diced zucchini

- 1 cup diced carrots

- 1 cup green beans, chopped

- 4 cups low-sodium turkey or chicken broth

Instructions:

1. Cook the ground turkey separately.

2. Dice the zucchini, carrots, and chop the green beans.

3. In the slow cooker, combine the cooked ground turkey, diced zucchini, diced carrots, chopped green beans, and low-sodium broth.

4. Mix well to combine all ingredients.

5. Set the slow cooker to low heat and cook for 6 hours.

6. Once cooked, allow the stew to cool before serving to your Rottweiler on a weight management diet.

Nutritional Information: Protein: 22g, Fat: 6g, Carbohydrates: 10g, Fiber: 3g, Calories: 170 per serving (serving size: 1 cup)

High Energy Beef and Quinoa Stew

Cooking Time: 8 hours on low

Servings: 6

Ingredients:

- 2 cups cubed beef stew meat

- 1 cup cooked quinoa

- 1 cup diced sweet potatoes

- 1 cup diced carrots

- 4 cups low-sodium beef broth

Instructions:

1. Cook the beef stew meat and quinoa separately.

2. Dice the sweet potatoes and carrots.

3. In the slow cooker, combine the cooked beef stew meat, cooked quinoa, diced sweet potatoes, diced carrots, and low-sodium beef broth.

4. Mix well to combine all ingredients.

5. Set the slow cooker to low heat and cook for 8 hours.

6. Once cooked, allow the stew to cool before serving to your high-energy Rottweiler.

Nutritional Information: Protein: 24g, Fat: 8g, Carbohydrates: 18g, Fiber: 4g, Calories: 220 per serving (serving size: 1 cup)

Joint Health Salmon and Sweet Potato Stew

Cooking Time: 6 hours on low

Servings: 8

Ingredients:

- 2 cups cooked salmon, flaked

- 1 cup diced sweet potatoes

- 1 cup diced carrots

- 1 cup diced celery

- 4 cups low-sodium fish or vegetable broth

Instructions:

1. Cook the salmon separately and flake it into small pieces.

2. Dice the sweet potatoes, carrots, and celery.

3. In the slow cooker, combine the cooked flaked salmon, diced sweet potatoes, diced carrots, diced celery, and low-sodium broth.

4. Mix well to combine all ingredients.

5. Set the slow cooker to low heat and cook for 6 hours.

6. Once cooked, allow the stew to cool before serving to your Rottweiler to support joint health.

Nutritional Information: Protein: 20g, Fat: 6g, Carbohydrates: 12g, Fiber: 3g, Calories: 180 per serving (serving size: 1 cup)

Digestive Health Chicken and Pumpkin Stew

Cooking Time: 6 hours on low

Servings: 8

Ingredients:

- 2 cups cooked shredded chicken

- 1 cup canned pumpkin puree

- 1 cup diced sweet potatoes

- 1 cup chopped spinach

- 4 cups low-sodium chicken broth

Instructions:

1. Cook the shredded chicken separately.

2. Dice the sweet potatoes and chop the spinach.

3. In the slow cooker, combine the cooked shredded chicken, canned pumpkin puree, diced sweet potatoes, chopped spinach, and low-sodium chicken broth.

4. Mix well to combine all ingredients.

5. Set the slow cooker to low heat and cook for 6 hours.

6. Once cooked, allow the stew to cool before serving to your Rottweiler to promote digestive health.

Nutritional Information: Protein: 18g, Fat: 4g, Carbohydrates: 10g, Fiber: 3g, Calories: 150 per serving (serving size: 1 cup)

Skin and Coat Health Salmon and Flaxseed Stew

Cooking Time: 6 hours on low

Servings: 8

Ingredients:

- 2 cups cooked salmon, flaked
- 1 cup diced sweet potatoes
- 1 cup diced carrots
- 1/4 cup ground flaxseed
- 4 cups low-sodium fish or vegetable broth

Instructions:

1. Cook the salmon separately and flake it into small pieces.
2. Dice the sweet potatoes and carrots.
3. In the slow cooker, combine the cooked flaked salmon, diced sweet potatoes, diced carrots, ground flaxseed, and low-sodium broth.
4. Mix well to combine all ingredients.
5. Set the slow cooker to low heat and cook for 6 hours.
6. Once cooked, allow the stew to cool before serving to your Rottweiler to support skin and coat health.

Nutritional Information: Protein: 20g, Fat: 6g, Carbohydrates: 12g, Fiber: 3g, Calories: 180 per serving (serving size: 1 cup)

Sensitive Skin Turkey and Oatmeal Stew

Cooking Time: 6 hours on low

Servings: 8

Ingredients:

- 2 cups cooked ground turkey

- 1 cup cooked oatmeal

- 1 cup diced sweet potatoes

- 1 cup diced zucchini

- 4 cups low-sodium turkey or chicken broth

Instructions:

1. Cook the ground turkey and oatmeal separately.

2. Dice the sweet potatoes and zucchini.

3. In the slow cooker, combine the cooked ground turkey, cooked oatmeal, diced sweet potatoes, diced zucchini, and low-sodium broth.

4. Mix well to combine all ingredients.

5. Set the slow cooker to low heat and cook for 6 hours.

6. Once cooked, allow the stew to cool before serving to your Rottweiler with sensitive skin.

Nutritional Information: Protein: 18g, Fat: 4g, Carbohydrates: 10g, Fiber: 3g, Calories: 150 per serving (serving size: 1 cup)

Low-Fat Diet Chicken and Vegetable Stew

Cooking Time: 6 hours on low

Servings: 8

Ingredients:

- 2 cups cooked shredded chicken
- 1 cup diced zucchini
- 1 cup diced carrots
- 1 cup chopped spinach
- 4 cups low-sodium chicken broth

Instructions:

1. Cook the shredded chicken separately.
2. Dice the zucchini and carrots, and chop the spinach.
3. In the slow cooker, combine the cooked shredded chicken, diced zucchini, diced carrots, chopped spinach, and low-sodium chicken broth.
4. Mix well to combine all ingredients.
5. Set the slow cooker to low heat and cook for 6 hours.
6. Once cooked, allow the stew to cool before serving to your Rottweiler on a low-fat diet.

Nutritional Information: Protein: 18g, Fat: 4g, Carbohydrates: 10g, Fiber: 3g, Calories: 150 per serving (serving size: 1 cup)

Grain-Free Diet Beef and Vegetable Stew

Cooking Time: 6 hours on low

Servings: 8

Ingredients:

- 2 cups cubed beef stew meat

- 1 cup diced sweet potatoes

- 1 cup diced carrots

- 1 cup chopped green beans

- 4 cups low-sodium beef broth

Instructions:

1. Cook the beef stew meat separately.

2. Dice the sweet potatoes and carrots, and chop the green beans.

3. In the slow cooker, combine the cooked beef stew meat, diced sweet potatoes, diced carrots, chopped green beans, and low-sodium broth.

4. Mix well to combine all ingredients.

5. Set the slow cooker to low heat and cook for 6 hours.

6. Once cooked, allow the stew to cool before serving to your Rottweiler on a grain-free diet.

Nutritional Information: Protein: 22g, Fat: 6g, Carbohydrates: 12g, Fiber: 3g, Calories: 170 per serving (serving size: 1 cup)

CONCLUSION

As we come to the end of this culinary journey tailored specifically for Rottweilers, I want to express my deepest gratitude for joining me on this adventure. Together, we've explored the transformative power of nutrition, delved into the intricacies of slow cooking for our beloved canine companions, and embarked on a quest for optimal health and well-being.

Throughout this cookbook, we've discovered a wealth of delicious and nourishing recipes designed to rejuvenate and revitalize our Rottweilers from the inside out. From hearty stews to savory treats, each dish has been crafted with care and consideration, with the sole purpose of enhancing the lives of our furry friends.

But our journey doesn't end here. As you venture into your kitchen to prepare these meals for your Rottweiler, I encourage you to embrace the process wholeheartedly. Take the time to savor each moment, to revel in the joy of creating something truly special for your beloved pet.

And as you do, I invite you to share your experiences with me. Your feedback, thoughts, and honest reviews are invaluable—they help me continue to improve and refine my recipes, ensuring that each and every Rottweiler receives the nourishment they deserve.

Together, let us continue to champion the health and happiness of our Rottweilers, one slow-cooked meal at a time. With your support and dedication, I have no doubt that we can make a meaningful difference in the lives of countless dogs around the world.

Thank you for entrusting me with the care of your furry companions. May your Rottweiler's tail wag with delight with each delicious bite, and may their health and vitality shine brighter than ever before.

BONUS 1
Training Tips and Tricks

Training your Rottweiler is an essential part of nurturing a strong and positive relationship with your canine companion. In this chapter, we'll explore effective training tips and tricks tailored specifically for Rottweilers, helping you establish clear communication, build trust, and instil good behaviour.

Understanding Your Rottweiler: Before diving into training techniques, it's crucial to understand the temperament and characteristics of Rottweilers. They are intelligent, loyal, and confident dogs with a natural inclination towards guarding and protecting. Rottweilers respond well to firm and consistent leadership, but they also thrive on positive reinforcement and rewards-based training methods.

Start Early: Training should begin as early as possible, ideally when your Rottweiler is a puppy. Early socialization and obedience training lay the foundation for a well-behaved and well-adjusted adult dog. Use positive experiences to introduce your Rottweiler to various people, animals, environments, and situations to prevent fearfulness and aggression later in life.

Basic Obedience Commands: Teaching basic obedience commands such as "sit," "stay," "come," "down," and "heel" is fundamental for effective communication and control. Use clear, consistent verbal cues and hand signals paired with rewards such as treats, praise, or toys to reinforce desired behaviours. Short, frequent training sessions throughout the day are more effective than lengthy sessions.

Positive Reinforcement: Rottweilers respond exceptionally well to positive reinforcement training methods. Reward desired behaviours immediately with treats, praise, or playtime to reinforce their understanding of what you expect from them. Consistency and patience are key; be sure to reward your Rottweiler every time they correctly execute a command.

Avoid Punishment: Avoid using harsh or punitive training methods with Rottweilers, as they can be counterproductive and damage the trust between you and your dog. Instead, focus on redirecting unwanted behaviours and providing alternative, acceptable outlets for their energy and instincts. Consistent reinforcement of desired behaviours will naturally diminish undesirable ones.

Socialization: Proper socialization is crucial for Rottweilers to develop into well-rounded and confident dogs. Expose them to various environments, people, animals, sounds, and experiences from a young age to prevent fearfulness and aggression. Supervise all interactions and ensure they remain positive and controlled.

Leash Training: Leash training is essential for Rottweilers, given their strength and size. Start leash training early and use positive reinforcement to teach them to walk calmly beside you without pulling. Consistency, patience, and frequent practice are key to mastering loose leash walking.

Behaviour Modification: Addressing undesirable behaviours such as jumping, barking, or chewing requires patience and consistency. Use redirection, positive reinforcement, and appropriate training techniques to modify behaviour effectively. Seek professional guidance if needed, especially for complex behavioural issues.

Advanced Training: Once your Rottweiler has mastered basic obedience commands, you can move on to more advanced training activities such as agility, obedience trials, or canine sports. These activities provide mental stimulation, physical exercise, and strengthen the bond between you and your dog.

Conclusion: Training your Rottweiler is a rewarding journey that requires dedication, patience, and understanding. By implementing positive reinforcement techniques, early socialization, and consistent training practices, you can cultivate a well-behaved, confident, and happy Rottweiler companion for years to come. Remember, training is an ongoing process that strengthens the bond between you and your dog while enriching both of your lives.

BONUS 2
30 Day Meal Plan

Day	Breakfast	Lunch	Dinner	Snacks
Day 1	Chicken and Rice Casserole	Turkey and Sweet Potato Stew	Beef and Vegetable Stew	Carrot Sticks
Day 2	Salmon and Oatmeal Patties	Chicken and Quinoa Soup	Turkey and Brown Rice Casserole	Apple Slices
Day 3	Beef and Pumpkin Muffins	Salmon and Green Bean Stew	Chicken and Lentil Curry	Blueberry Treats
Day 4	Turkey and Cranberry Bars	Beef and Carrot Biscuits	Salmon and Spinach Risotto	Peanut Butter Kong Stuffing
Day 5	Chicken and Sweet Potato Hash	Turkey and Barley Stew	Beef and Pea Stew	Frozen Banana Slices
Day 6	Salmon and Broccoli Frittata	Chicken and Rice Congee	Turkey and Potato Bake	Frozen Green Bean Chews
Day 7	Beef and Carrot Omelette	Salmon and Pumpkin Chowder	Chicken and Zucchini Casserole	Yogurt Drops

Day 8	Turkey and Spinach Breakfast Muffins	Beef and Sweet Potato Curry	Salmon and Quinoa Pilaf	Carrot and Apple Slices
Day 9	Chicken and Brown Rice Porridge	Turkey and Green Bean Stew	Beef and Lentil Soup	Frozen Blueberries
Day 10	Salmon and Potato Pancakes	Chicken and Carrot Casserole	Turkey and Barley Risotto	Watermelon Cubes
Day 11	Beef and Pea Frittata	Salmon and Broccoli Risotto	Chicken and Spinach Stew	Cottage Cheese
Day 12	Turkey and Pumpkin Breakfast Bars	Beef and Rice Pilaf	Salmon and Sweet Potato Stew	Frozen Peas
Day 13	Chicken and Barley Porridge	Turkey and Quinoa Soup	Beef and Green Bean Casserole	Apple Slices with Peanut Butter
Day 14	Salmon and Spinach Omelette	Chicken and Potato Bake	Turkey and Lentil Curry	Frozen Carrot Coins
Day 15	Beef and Carrot Pancakes	Salmon and Pea Stew	Chicken and Brown Rice Casserole	Blueberry Frozen Yogurt
Day 16	Turkey and Green Bean Frittata	Beef and Potato Chowder	Salmon and Barley Risotto	Frozen Watermelon Cubes

Day 17	Chicken and Sweet Potato Breakfast Muffins	Turkey and Lentil Soup	Beef and Broccoli Casserole	Green Beans with Peanut Butter
Day 18	Salmon and Quinoa Porridge	Chicken and Spinach Stew	Turkey and Green Bean Bake	Apple Slices with Cottage Cheese
Day 19	Beef and Pumpkin Omelette	Salmon and Brown Rice Casserole	Chicken and Barley Pilaf	Frozen Blueberry and Yogurt Treats
Day 20	Turkey and Potato Pancakes	Beef and Lentil Curry	Salmon and Carrot Stew	Frozen Pea Pops
Day 21	Chicken and Rice Patties	Turkey and Vegetable Risotto	Beef and Sweet Potato Bake	Carrot Sticks with Peanut Butter
Day 22	Salmon and Green Bean Omelette	Chicken and Broccoli Soup	Turkey and Spinach Casserole	Frozen Banana Chunks
Day 23	Beef and Barley Porridge	Salmon and Potato Stew	Chicken and Pea Risotto	Watermelon Cubes with Cottage Cheese
Day 24	Turkey and Sweet Potato Breakfast Bars	Beef and Green Bean Casserole	Salmon and Lentil Soup	Blueberry Frozen Yogurt Treats
Day 25	Chicken and Quinoa Pancakes	Turkey and Carrot Stew	Beef and Potato Bake	Frozen Green Beans

Day 26	Salmon and Spinach Breakfast Muffins	Chicken and Brown Rice Risotto	Turkey and Broccoli Casserole	Apple Slices with Peanut Butter
Day 27	Beef and Pumpkin Pancakes	Salmon and Barley Pilaf	Chicken and Potato Chowder	Frozen Carrot Coins
Day 28	Turkey and Pea Porridge	Beef and Sweet Potato Casserole	Salmon and Green Bean Stew	Blueberry Frozen Yogurt Treats
Day 29	Chicken and Lentil Patties	Turkey and Spinach Soup	Beef and Carrot Risotto	Frozen Watermelon Cubes
Day 30	Salmon and Potato Breakfast Muffins	Chicken and Quinoa Stew	Turkey and Brown Rice Chowder	Carrot Sticks with Cottage Cheese

MEAL PLANNER JOURNAL

WEEKLY —

Meal Planner

Week of:

Monday	Tuesday	Wednesday
BREAKFAST	BREAKFAST	BREAKFAST
LUNCH	LUNCH	LUNCH
DINNER	DINNER	DINNER
SNACK	SNACK	SNACK

Thursday	Friday	Saturday
BREAKFAST	BREAKFAST	BREAKFAST
LUNCH	LUNCH	LUNCH
DINNER	DINNER	DINNER
SNACK	SNACK	SNACK

Sunday	NOTES:
BREAKFAST	
LUNCH	
DINNER	
SNACK	

Meal Planner

Week of:

Monday	**Tuesday**	**Wednesday**
BREAKFAST	BREAKFAST	BREAKFAST
LUNCH	LUNCH	LUNCH
DINNER	DINNER	DINNER
SNACK	SNACK	SNACK

Thursday	**Friday**	**Saturday**
BREAKFAST	BREAKFAST	BREAKFAST
LUNCH	LUNCH	LUNCH
DINNER	DINNER	DINNER
SNACK	SNACK	SNACK

Sunday	**NOTES:**
BREAKFAST	
LUNCH	
DINNER	
SNACK	

Meal Planner

Week of:

Monday	**Tuesday**	**Wednesday**
BREAKFAST	BREAKFAST	BREAKFAST
LUNCH	LUNCH	LUNCH
DINNER	DINNER	DINNER
SNACK	SNACK	SNACK
Thursday	**Friday**	**Saturday**
BREAKFAST	BREAKFAST	BREAKFAST
LUNCH	LUNCH	LUNCH
DINNER	DINNER	DINNER
SNACK	SNACK	SNACK

Sunday	NOTES:
BREAKFAST	
LUNCH	
DINNER	
SNACK	

Meal Planner

Week of:

Monday	**Tuesday**	**Wednesday**
BREAKFAST	BREAKFAST	BREAKFAST
LUNCH	LUNCH	LUNCH
DINNER	DINNER	DINNER
SNACK	SNACK	SNACK
Thursday	**Friday**	**Saturday**
BREAKFAST	BREAKFAST	BREAKFAST
LUNCH	LUNCH	LUNCH
DINNER	DINNER	DINNER
SNACK	SNACK	SNACK

Sunday	NOTES:
BREAKFAST	
LUNCH	
DINNER	
SNACK	

Meal Planner

Week of:

Monday	Tuesday	Wednesday
BREAKFAST	BREAKFAST	BREAKFAST
LUNCH	LUNCH	LUNCH
DINNER	DINNER	DINNER
SNACK	SNACK	SNACK

Thursday	Friday	Saturday
BREAKFAST	BREAKFAST	BREAKFAST
LUNCH	LUNCH	LUNCH
DINNER	DINNER	DINNER
SNACK	SNACK	SNACK

Sunday	NOTES:
BREAKFAST	
LUNCH	
DINNER	
SNACK	

Meal Planner

Week of:

Monday

BREAKFAST

LUNCH

DINNER

SNACK

Tuesday

BREAKFAST

LUNCH

DINNER

SNACK

Wednesday

BREAKFAST

LUNCH

DINNER

SNACK

Thursday

BREAKFAST

LUNCH

DINNER

SNACK

Friday

BREAKFAST

LUNCH

DINNER

SNACK

Saturday

BREAKFAST

LUNCH

DINNER

SNACK

Sunday

BREAKFAST

LUNCH

DINNER

SNACK

NOTES:

Meal Planner

Week of:

Monday	Tuesday	Wednesday
BREAKFAST	BREAKFAST	BREAKFAST
LUNCH	LUNCH	LUNCH
DINNER	DINNER	DINNER
SNACK	SNACK	SNACK

Thursday	Friday	Saturday
BREAKFAST	BREAKFAST	BREAKFAST
LUNCH	LUNCH	LUNCH
DINNER	DINNER	DINNER
SNACK	SNACK	SNACK

Sunday	NOTES:
BREAKFAST	
LUNCH	
DINNER	
SNACK	

Meal Planner

Week of:

Monday	Tuesday	Wednesday
BREAKFAST	BREAKFAST	BREAKFAST
LUNCH	LUNCH	LUNCH
DINNER	DINNER	DINNER
SNACK	SNACK	SNACK

Thursday	Friday	Saturday
BREAKFAST	BREAKFAST	BREAKFAST
LUNCH	LUNCH	LUNCH
DINNER	DINNER	DINNER
SNACK	SNACK	SNACK

Sunday	NOTES:
BREAKFAST	
LUNCH	
DINNER	
SNACK	

Meal Planner

Week of:

Monday	**Tuesday**	**Wednesday**
BREAKFAST	BREAKFAST	BREAKFAST
LUNCH	LUNCH	LUNCH
DINNER	DINNER	DINNER
SNACK	SNACK	SNACK
Thursday	**Friday**	**Saturday**
BREAKFAST	BREAKFAST	BREAKFAST
LUNCH	LUNCH	LUNCH
DINNER	DINNER	DINNER
SNACK	SNACK	SNACK

Sunday

BREAKFAST

LUNCH

DINNER

SNACK

NOTES:

Meal Planner

Week of:

Monday	Tuesday	Wednesday
BREAKFAST	BREAKFAST	BREAKFAST
LUNCH	LUNCH	LUNCH
DINNER	DINNER	DINNER
SNACK	SNACK	SNACK

Thursday	Friday	Saturday
BREAKFAST	BREAKFAST	BREAKFAST
LUNCH	LUNCH	LUNCH
DINNER	DINNER	DINNER
SNACK	SNACK	SNACK

Sunday	NOTES:
BREAKFAST	
LUNCH	
DINNER	
SNACK	

Meal Planner

Month of:

Sun	Mon	Tues	Wed	Thurs	Fri	Sat